Everything You Need To Know About

ALCOHOL

Teens often feel pressured to drink with friends.

• THE NEED TO KNOW LIBRARY •

Everything You Need To Know About

ALCOHOL

Barbara Taylor

Series Editor: Evan Stark, Ph.D.

THE ROSEN PUBLISHING GROUP, INC.
NEW YORK

Published in 1989, 1993, 1996 by The Rosen Publishing Group, Inc.
29 East 21st Street, New York, NY 10010

Revised Edition 1996
Copyright © 1989, 1993, 1996 by The Rosen Publishing Group, Inc.

Manufactured in the United States of America.

Library of Congress Cataloging-in-Publication Data

Taylor, Barbara, 1938–
    Everying you need to know about alcohol/ Barbara Taylor
    (The need to know library)
    Includes bibliographical references and index.
    Summary: Describes the effects of alcohol on mind and body and
directs those in jeopardy to seek help.
    ISBN 0-8239-2316-9
    1. Alcoholism—Juvenile literature.   2. Alcohol—Physiological effect—
Juvenile literature. [1. Alcoholism] I. Title. II. Title: Alcohol.
III. Series.
RC565.T38 1988
613.8′1—dc19   89-39820
                                                 CIP
                                                 AC

Contents

Introduction

Ifyou are old enough to be reading this book, chances are you have had some experience with alcohol. Maybe you've tried it. Or maybe your friends have. You've probably seen your parents or other adults drinking it. How do you feel about alcohol?

One thing you should realize is that alcohol is a drug. It's hard to think of it in that way. Cocaine is a drug. Heroin is a drug. But alcohol? Most people don't see it that way because it is a legal drug, like caffeine. But it is a substance that affects the body in very specific ways. As you grow older, you will encounter alcohol more and more often, so you should be aware of how this drug can affect you and those around you.

It is especially important to be aware of the dangers of drinking alcohol. You should know that drinking and driving kills more than 3,600 teens and injures nearly 85,000 more teens in the United States each year. Drunk driving is the leading cause of motor vehicle deaths in North America. A drunk driver runs the risk of killing or injuring other people without even realizing it. See pages 28–30 for more information on drunk driving.

So what if you just drink without driving? Well, that can cause problems, too. One in five American teens has a drinking problem. Like any other drug, you can become addicted to alcohol. That means you lose control of yourself and cannot stop drinking. **Alcoholism** is a disease that can take away everything that is important to you. Chapters 5 to 7 deal specifically with this problem.

As a young man or woman, you probably have many exciting plans for your future. No matter what those plans may be, alcohol abuse is something that can get in your way. It can slow you down, or stop you completely. It is not easy to recognize a drinking problem in yourself, and many young people don't realize it until it is too late. Educate yourself about the risks before you decide to drink.

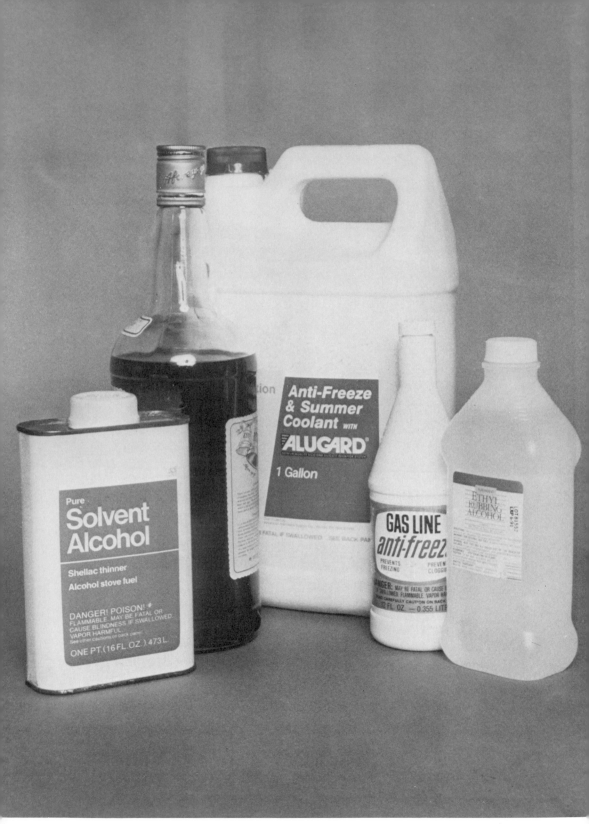

There are many kinds of alcohol. Each has a variety of uses.

Chapter 1

All About Alcohol

Alcohol can be found in many things besides beverages. Did you ever wonder if that stuff in your medicine cabinet could make a person drunk? Actually, that kind of alcohol is poisonous; it can seriously harm you or even kill you. It is called **methyl** alcohol, and it is used in cleaning solutions, paint removers, antifreeze, shaving lotions, and hair sprays. (None of these things make very good drinks.)

To dissolve paint or tar, **amyl** or **propyl** alcohol should do the trick. To paint lines on a highway or kill insects, use **butyl** alcohol (or **butanol**). Also deadly is **denatured** alcohol, to which poisons have been added; it is used for paints and dyes and for cleaning the skin.

The beverage alcohol is **ethyl** alcohol. This is the alcohol we will be talking about.

Making Alcohol

Ethyl alcohol is made by fermentation. In this process the starch and sugar in natural products such as potatoes, fruits (grapes, apples, plums), and grains (barley, rye, corn, wheat) are changed into ethyl alcohol.

You may have seen the result of fermentation. Did you ever leave milk out of the refrigerator overnight in a warm room? Fermentation caused the milk to smell and taste different.

Yeast causes these changes. Yeast plants travel in the air. They are so tiny that they are invisible to the naked eye. They land on the warm milk.

Beer

The process of making beer is called **brewing**. In brewing, a liquid mixture of yeast is added to a mixture of malted cereals (barley, rye, corn, wheat, and others). The yeast ferments the grain, changing it to alcohol. When fermentation stops, the liquid is beer. Tiny dried flower buds called hops are added to the liquid for flavor. Hops also help preserve the beer.

Ale is made from the same ingredients as beer. The alcoholic content of ale is slightly higher.

Light beer has fewer calories and a lower alcoholic content than regular beer.

Dark beer (stout, bock beer, porter) is named for its darker color. Dark beers contain more alco-

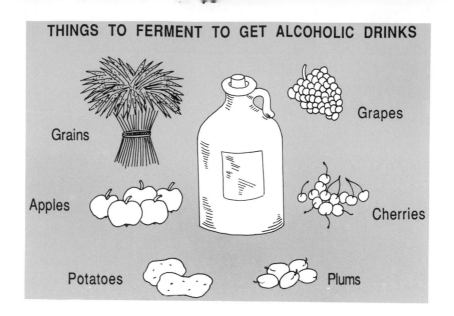

THINGS TO FERMENT TO GET ALCOHOLIC DRINKS

Grains

Grapes

Apples

Cherries

Potatoes

Plums

hol than most other beers. The taste of dark beer is stronger and sweeter.

Three point two beer (sometimes called three-two beer) contains no more than 3.2 percent alcohol. In some areas teens can buy 3.2 beer before they reach the legal drinking age.

Nonalcoholic beer is also available today. It looks like other beers, but offers refreshment without the effects of alcohol.

Wine

Wine is also made by natural fermentation. Most wines are made from grapes. But some wines are made from other fruits and even from vegetables.

Wine makers add yeast to warm fruit or vegetable juice. The yeast changes the sugar in the juice. The change produces alcohol and a gas called **carbon dioxide**. The gas is allowed to escape. The juice ferments. When fermentation stops, the juice is wine.

11

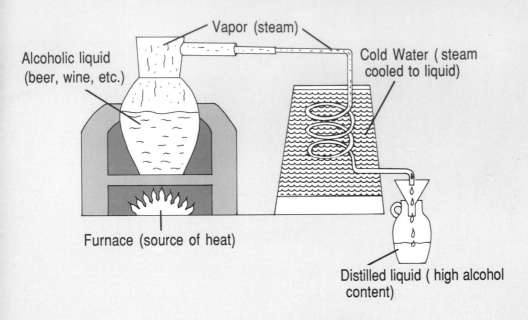

DISTILLATION PROCESS FOR MAKING ALCOHOL

Vapor (steam)

Alcoholic liquid (beer, wine, etc.)

Cold Water (steam cooled to liquid)

Furnace (source of heat)

Distilled liquid (high alcohol content)

Wines can be white, red, or rosé, depending on the kind of grape that is used. Wine is **sweet** or **dry**. A wine can be sweetened with unfermented sugar. Dry wines contain only a small amount of sugar. Wines can be **carbonated**. These are called **sparkling wines**. Carbon dioxide is added after fermentation to give the wine its bubbles. Champagne is a sparkling wine. Madeira, port, and sherry are **fortified** wines. They contain more alcohol than other wines.

Liquor

Whiskey, rum, vodka, gin, brandy, and stronger alcoholic beverages are made by **distillation**. The fermented liquid is heated in a machine called a still. The industrial plant where liquor is made is called a distillery.

In distillation, a fermented liquid that contains alcohol is heated. The alcohol in the wine or beer **vaporizes**. That means it becomes steam. The steam is collected and cooled. As the steam cools, it becomes a liquid that is nearly pure alcohol. Flavorings and water are added to this alcohol.

Some of the popular distilled beverages are:

- **Whiskey** (rye, scotch, bourbon): made by distilling the fermented juice of cereal grains such as rye, corn, or barley.
- **Gin:** made by distilling rye and other grains and flavoring the alcohol with juniper berries.
- **Vodka:** distilled from rye malt, fermented potatoes, or fruit such as apples.
- **Rum:** made from fermented molasses or the juice of sugarcane.
- **Brandy:** distilled from wine. It can be made from grapes and other fruits such as plums, apples, cherries, and apricots.
- **Liqueurs:** distilled beverages made by adding fruit and herbs to brandy. People usually drink them after dinner.

Alcohol Is Fattening

All alcohol, fermented or distilled, contains calories. The body oxidizes it—unites it with oxygen. This process produces energy, so alcohol provides the body with calories. One ounce of alcohol has about 160 calories.

Providing fattening calories is all that alcohol does for the body. Alcohol contains no nutrients, vitamins, or minerals.

Alcohol as a Drug

When people hear the word "drug," they usually think of illegal street drugs such as marijuana, heroin, or cocaine. Sometimes they think of prescription medicines—the drugs that doctors prescribe to help patients get well. People seldom think of alcohol when they hear the word "drug." But alcohol *is* a drug—the most widely used drug in the world.

Like all drugs, alcohol causes changes in the human body. Alcohol acts as a depressant on the body's nervous system. A depressant slows a person down.

Watch someone who has had quite a bit to drink in a short time. You will see the depressant at work. You will notice the drinker's speech becoming slurred. You will see that his or her steps become unsteady. Toss a ball toward the drinker, and he or she will probably have trouble catching it. A person's reflexes become dulled when the nervous system slows down.

Why Is Alcohol Legal?

Most drugs are not legal. To buy them, people

After a few drinks, even simple tasks can become difficult.

need permission from a doctor. But it is legal, for those over twenty-one, to buy and to drink alcohol.

Alcohol is different from other drugs such as heroin and cocaine because people can drink alcohol without necessarily becoming addicted. Alcohol does not necessarily cause addiction (physical need for a drug) or dependency (strong desire to take a drug often). It does cause addiction in some people who are called **alcoholics**. An alcoholic is a person who has the disease called **alcoholism**. Alcoholics cannot control their need for alcohol. And when they drink, they cannot stop.

Some people think alcohol should not be legal. They point to the millions of alcoholics and the great number of deaths caused by drinking and driving. There was a short period in the United

States when alcohol was illegal. In 1919 Congress passed the Eighteenth Amendment to the Constitution, called the Prohibition Amendment. It forbade the making, drinking, and sale of alcohol. But in 1933, due to public protest and the ineffectiveness of Prohibition, Congress passed the Repeal Amendment, which reversed the law. People had decided that they wanted to choose whether to drink or not.

Just the Facts

- **About 11 million people in the United States are alcoholics.** Over 3 million of those are between the ages twelve and seventeen.
- **Alcohol is the third highest cause of death in the United States.** It kills 205,000 people a year.
- **Alcohol harms drinkers.** Alcohol is involved in 33 percent of all suicides, 50 percent of all fatal falls, and 68 percent of all deaths by drowning.
- **Alcohol harms nondrinkers.** Other people's drinking problems have harmed about 41 percent of the adult population. Alcohol is involved in 80 percent of all fires, 64 percent of all murders, and 60 percent of child abuse. Alcoholism costs United States businesses about $43 billion a year.

Chapter 2

What's Your Point of View?

*"H*e's just an old drunk."

"She doesn't drink, she doesn't smoke. What does she do?"

"That stuff is poison. It'll kill you."

"Hey, relax. Have a drink!"

People hold many views about alcohol. Some see it as the only way to party. Others think of it as a tool of the devil. Many people are not sure. Nondrinkers sometimes have negative feelings toward those who drink, while some drinkers are uncomfortable with people who do not drink. Whether drinking is or is not harmful, everybody should be given the right to express their opinion.

Like most things, if we do not talk openly about alcohol, we will never learn anything about it. There are no wrong opinions, just wise and unwise choices. We learn how to make wise choices by educating ourselves and sharing ideas with others.

Second Thoughts

"So what do you want to do tonight?" asked Marco. He and his friend, Alex, were lying on the floor of his living room, flipping through channels with the television remote control. "I don't know," said Alex. "What is there to do?"

"Nothing," Marco replied. "My parents will be here all night."

Alex stared at the ceiling and said, "Well, we could go to Chief's..."

Marco snickered. "Alex, we're sixteen," he said. "We'd never get in."

Alex frowned. "Well, we could try," he said. "I want to get drunk tonight. Don't you?"

"I don't know," Marco said cautiously. "I don't think I'm really into it anymore."

Marco and Alex had been getting drunk together almost every weekend for the past three months. They got alcohol anywhere and everywhere they could. They stole it from their parents or paid older kids to buy it for them. It seemed exciting and kind of grown-up to get wasted on Saturday nights.

"What do you mean, you're not into it?" Alex demanded, sitting up.

"I mean, I'm getting kind of sick of it," said Marco. "I don't want to get addicted, plus I feel so tired and gross during the week."

It's all right to refuse a drink.

"Marco, we live in a really boring city. What is there for people our age to do, besides going to lame mixers?" said Alex.

Marco glanced cautiously at Alex. "I'm sure we could find something else to do besides getting drunk every weekend," he said. "Maybe you have a drinking problem and don't even know it."

"Oh, please. Like, okay Nancy Reagan, I'll say no to drinking," Alex scoffed.

Marco sat up and looked at Alex. "Look, I think I should stop," he said. "I don't want to drink anymore. You can do it all you want, but I'm done."

Alex sighed. "Marco, you're being such a total drag. Don't you want to have fun anymore?"

Marco shrugged and said, "I need a break, okay? When are we ever going to start that band we used to talk about? You lost interest when we started getting drunk all the time."

"I don't want to start some stupid band," Alex said. "I want to party."

It can be hard to stand up to friends when it comes to drinking. Peer pressure is complicated and hard to deal with. But it is important to express how you feel, even if you know your friends don't agree. Trust your instincts, use your head, and express yourself.

Listening to Yourself

Teens are often bombarded by many mixed

Drinking alcohol can cause depression.

messages about alcohol. You may get warnings
about its dangers at school, or from your parents.

But many messages about alcohol come from
advertising. Think of all of the beer commercials
you have seen. Don't they make drinking beer
seem like fun? The ads seem to suggest that if you
drink beer, you will end up at a fabulous party on a
tropical island, surrounded by beautiful people in
swimwear.

Of course, it never happens that way in real life.
But advertising sends this message to you all the
time. The next time you watch those commercials,
try to look closely at how they are trying to
influence you. That will help you to make up your
own mind.

You may also see adults behave badly when they drink, perhaps by being rude or driving drunk. Remember, adults are not always right. If you see adults acting this way, do not follow their example; you may have better judgment than they do.

As a teenager, you should be aware of your own values. Think about what you believe is right or wrong. Try to remember those values when you must decide about your own behavior.

Using What You've Learned

Imagine that your friend Darnell asks you for some advice:

Darnell: *Hey, man, I need your opinion. Listen, I don't drink. But I met this girl, and I really like her. She's hot. We really hit it off and everything, but like, I'm pretty sure she gets drunk a lot. She talks about getting trashed, and I think she wants me to do it with her. We're supposed to go to this party Saturday. I think it's a keg party. If I don't drink, will everyone think I'm a total freak? Or, like, is that cool? I could say I'm driving or something. But she'll know I don't have a car. Should I tell her I don't drink? Is she gonna hate me, or what? What should I do?*

What would you tell Darnell? Should he drink, even though he doesn't want to? Should he be honest with the girl? Think about it.

Tina: *I still can't believe I'm hanging out with Jill and Heather. I mean, they are really cool, but I always thought they had no idea who I was. Now we're friends. You should go out with us some time. They'd like you. The only thing is, I had no idea how much booze those girls put away! They drink all the time, and so now I drink all the time. I mean, what else can I do? If I didn't drink, they probably wouldn't hang out with me. I know I shouldn't be doing it, but . . . I like them. They're my friends, and we have fun getting plastered together. I don't know. What do you think?*

Would you tell Tina to keep drinking so she could be friends with Jill and Heather? Would they understand if she stopped? Is it worth it?

For many people, social drinking means having one or two alcoholic drinks.

Chapter 3

Why Does Anybody Drink?

After being warned so strongly about the dangers of alcohol, you may wonder why people still drink. You may wonder why it is legal, and if it is even possible to drink responsibly. Actually, many adults over the age of twenty-one can drink in small quantities and maintain control.

Under Control

When it is kept to a minimum, drinking can make an adult social drinker feel relaxed. Some types of alcohol do taste good (although most of them take some getting used to). For these reasons, adults sometimes drink in groups. Many people think that it helps them to loosen up and have a good time, although anybody can also do that without alcohol.

Most of these drinkers can continue drinking socially without becoming addicted. But if a social drinker loses that control, he or she could become an alcoholic.

Nondrinkers

People who do not drink any alcohol at all are called "abstainers" or "teetotalers." Nondrinkers have various reasons for making the choice not to use alcohol.

People often abstain from drinking because of their religious beliefs. Many religions teach their followers to abstain from alcohol completely. There are some religious people who believe that **no one** should drink alcohol.

Some people do not drink because they know that they cannot control the use of alcohol. This is true of anyone who is an alcoholic. An alcoholic who understands this and avoids all alcohol is making a good choice—a choice that could save his or her life.

People also avoid alcohol because they simply do not like the taste or the feeling it gives them. Some people are even **allergic** to alcohol. Being allergic to something means that your body does not react well to the substance.

Teenage Drinking

Teenagers often want to drink alcohol to appear more grown-up. Sometimes they are curious about drinking. Or they just want to fit in with the crowd. But the problems drinking can cause for teenagers are probably even harder to handle than the problems adults face.

In every state in the United States, teenagers cannot drink without breaking the law. Selling alcoholic beverages to people under the legal drinking age is a crime. Serving alcoholic beverages to that group is also a crime. Even parents who allow their children to serve alcoholic beverages at parties are breaking the law.

Being responsible about drinking is difficult. It involves judgment and maturity. It calls for an understanding of your own body and how it reacts to alcohol. And it requires the courage to be able to say no to something—even if all your friends are doing it. This is a big job. That is why state laws require teens to wait.

Health experts, too, have reason to be concerned. They have found that the younger a person starts drinking, the more likely it is that he or she will drink heavily as an adult.

According to recent surveys, young people today start drinking at an earlier age and more often than young people did in past years.

Beer and wine are usually the first drinks sampled by young people. Their first taste of alcohol may be a glass of wine at dinner. Or they may have wine at a religious service, or as a toast at a party.

Experts say that the reason for the trend toward early drinking is strong pressure from friends. A survey of more than 500,000 schoolchildren in the United States shows the following facts about young people and alcohol:

• About one-third of all fourth graders (34 percent) report that they are pressured by kids their age to try beer, wine, or liquor.
• Nine out of ten children in grades four, five, and six are aware that cocaine and marijuana are drugs. Less than five out of ten call alcohol a drug. Only one in five thinks of wine coolers as a drug. A wine cooler is a bottled mixture of wine and soda.

It can be hard for young people to say no to alcohol. But it is very important to be able to do it. Public health experts say that their studies show important things. Young people who drink alcohol regularly are taking real chances with their health. And they are taking risks with their future too. These young people often perform poorly in school. They become involved in crimes and accidents more often than others in their age group.

Teenage Drinking and Driving

An area of alcohol abuse that seriously affects teenagers is drunken driving. Pediatricians (doctors of children, preteens, and teenagers) report that the leading cause of death for young adults aged fifteen to twenty-four years is driving under the influence of alcohol.

It is dangerous to drink and drive.

Some young people tend to take more risks when driving than adults do. Drunk driving is a risk not worth taking for anyone, but it can be especially dangerous for young people inexperienced in driving.

Prom Night

Janet had been planning for prom night all week. She was excited, but not entirely about the dance. She saw it more as a night to get dressed up and party with her friends. Her date was Reggie, one of her best friends from school. They planned on getting wasted before the dance, going there and being obnoxious for about twenty minutes. Then they were going back to Reggie's and drink some more, since his parents were out of town.

Reggie picked Janet up at 7:30. They got into his car, and he immediately popped open a beer. "We're starting now?" asked Janet, startled.

"We have to, darling," said Reggie. "We can get trashed on the way to school. Beth and Tony will already be messed up when we meet them there."

Janet cautiously agreed and opened her own beer.

Before they were even halfway to the school, Reggie had downed two beers and was working on his third. Suddenly Janet noticed him swerving. "You idiot!" she screamed, grabbing the wheel. Reggie couldn't stop laughing as they straightened out on the road. Janet wasn't laughing, even though she was pretty buzzed herself.

They were moving pretty fast now. "Reggie, you're doing sixty! Slow down, okay?" pleaded Janet. Then she saw the red light.

Reggie slammed on the brakes, but the car skidded into the intersection. Another car slammed into the driver's side, and Reggie was killed instantly. Janet and the driver of the other car were seriously injured.

Chapter 4

The Effects of Alcohol on the Human Body

Alcohol affects everyone who drinks it—men and women, old and young, experienced drinkers, and people who drink for the first time.

Alcohol makes everyone who drinks it "feel different." One drink may make a person feel relaxed or happy. Or the person may simply feel different. A second drink may begin to slow the drinker down. More drinks may cause the drinker to fall asleep (pass out). A lot of liquor will result in a medical emergency for the drinker.

The reason a person is drinking also affects the drinker. Some reasons for drinking are appropriate. Others are not and may lead to problems.

The effects of alcohol differ from person to person. The effects may depend on the person's body size. Generally, the larger the person, the more blood the person has to contain the alcohol. A small teenager will feel the effect of alcohol more quickly and strongly than a large adult. The teenager has less blood than the adult.

The type of drink also makes a difference. Alcoholic beverages contain different amounts of alcohol. A person who drinks four ounces of liquor takes in more alcohol than a person who drinks four ounces of beer.

The size of the drink is a factor. The more alcohol in a drink, the stronger the effects of that drink will be.

The length of time taken to drink makes a difference. An adult can probably handle four drinks over six hours. But if the adult has four drinks in one hour, he or she will most certainly feel the effects.

The amount of food in the stomach makes a difference too. A person gets drunk more quickly on an empty stomach.

How a person is feeling when he or she drinks makes a difference. If a person drinks while tense, angry, uncomfortable, or tired from work, chances are that the effects of alcohol will be stronger. A problem is less likely if a person is comfortable and relaxed.

Another factor is "drug sensitivity." Some people are affected strongly by small amounts of alcohol, other drugs, and even medicines.

All of these factors affect how a person reacts, so it is easy to see how alcohol can affect people differently. Two people drinking the same drink can feel it differently. And the same drink on

AREAS OF THE BODY AFFECTED BY ALCOHOL

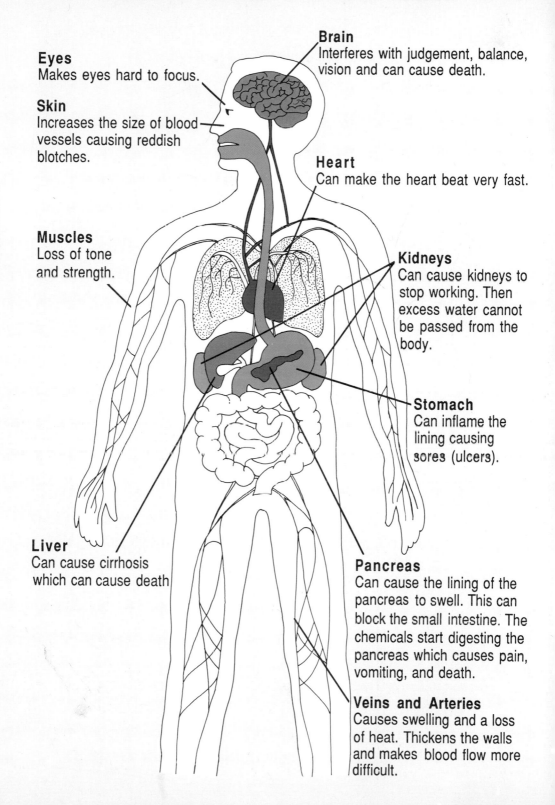

Eyes
Makes eyes hard to focus.

Skin
Increases the size of blood vessels causing reddish blotches.

Brain
Interferes with judgement, balance, vision and can cause death.

Heart
Can make the heart beat very fast.

Muscles
Loss of tone and strength.

Kidneys
Can cause kidneys to stop working. Then excess water cannot be passed from the body.

Stomach
Can inflame the lining causing sores (ulcers).

Liver
Can cause cirrhosis which can cause death

Pancreas
Can cause the lining of the pancreas to swell. This can block the small intestine. The chemicals start digesting the pancreas which causes pain, vomiting, and death.

Veins and Arteries
Causes swelling and a loss of heat. Thickens the walls and makes blood flow more difficult.

two occasions can affect the same person differently.

How Alcohol Affects the Body

Alcohol is a drug. It has a physical effect on every organ in the body from the moment it enters the system. Twenty percent of the alcohol taken into the body passes through the stomach into the bloodstream. It is carried in the bloodstream throughout the body.

The blood carries the alcohol to the brain. After one or two drinks, the drinker may feel warm and relaxed. After three or four drinks, speech becomes slurred and walking becomes difficult. The drinker has trouble focusing his eyes. After additional drinks, the drinker may not be able to talk or walk well.

If still more alcohol is put into the body, the drinker may pass out. The alcohol has depressed the workings of the brain.

The heavy drinker often feels the effects of alcohol the next morning. The drinker suffers a **hangover**. This means that he or she feels sick and may experience a headache. The pounding headache is caused by overexpanded blood vessels in the brain.

A hangover lasts until the alcohol is completely out of the body. There is no fast cure for a hangover. Suggested cures such as black coffee, a cold shower, or physical workouts do not work. The only way to cure a hangover is to get sober. And that takes time.

The best way to avoid a hangover is not to drink alcohol.

How the Body Gets Rid of Alcohol

The body gets rid of alcohol in two ways: **elimination** and **oxidation**. Elimination gets rid of a small amount of the alcohol in the body; oxidation gets rid of most of it.

Elimination

The body eliminates most of the alcohol through the kidneys. The alcohol passes out of the body in urine.

A small amount of the alcohol is eliminated through the lungs. The blood carries the alcohol to the lungs, and there it is exhaled. A person who is drinking can have "whiskey breath." This is the result of alcohol evaporation when the person breathes out.

Perspiration also helps the body get rid of alcohol. Some alcohol leaves the body through the sweat glands.

Oxidation

Oxidation is the joining of a substance with oxygen. Through oxidation, the body burns off alcohol. In the body, alcohol is joined with carbon dioxide and water. Oxidation occurs mainly in the

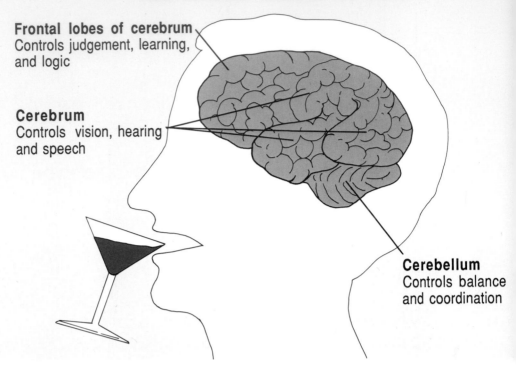

Frontal lobes of cerebrum
Controls judgement, learning, and logic

Cerebrum
Controls vision, hearing and speech

Cerebellum
Controls balance and coordination

liver. But the liver can handle only a small amount of alcohol each hour. So most of the alcohol must stay in the bloodstream. It continues to flow to the organs, cells, and tissues of the body. It circulates until the liver can get rid of it. A person who drinks more alcohol in an hour than the liver can handle in that time will feel drunk.

Elimination and oxidation are the only ways the body can get rid of alcohol. Both processes take time.

How Alcohol Harms the Body

People who drink too much over a long period of time will find that alcohol can harm their health. This can happen even if they are not alcoholics.

Three to four drinks a day on a regular basis can harm an adult body.

Large amounts of alcohol can harm the heart, veins, and arteries. Alcohol can thicken the walls of the arteries, raising the blood pressure. Alcohol causes the heart to beat faster, which can be dangerous for a person with heart disease.

Alcohol can cause kidney damage. If the kidneys fail, a person may die. A disease called **cirrhosis** of the liver is often fatal. It strikes people who drink a lot of alcohol.

A woman who drinks at all during pregnancy passes the alcohol along to the fetus (unborn child) in her body. The alcohol affects the fetus too. The fetus of a woman who drinks during pregnancy is at risk. The baby could be born deformed or with heart problems. Many children born to mothers who drink alcohol are born small. They may not grow or develop normally. They may have learning problems later in life.

Alcohol abuse can injure the brain centers that control learning, judgment, and social actions. Large doses of alcohol can injure the parts of the brain that control breathing and heartbeat. Too much alcohol in the brain can cause death.

Alcohol can affect a heavy drinker in other ways, too. A person who is drunk can be aggressive, or tense, or depressed. These conditions can result in accidents, even suicide. They can destroy friendships and family life.

Too much alcohol can make a person aggressive.

Alcohol use does not harm everyone's health. Most people can drink a small to moderate amount of alcohol on occasion. It will not cause them any harm.

But for some people, *any* amount of alcohol is harmful. These include people who have trouble with their heart, liver, stomach, or other organs. And there is another group of people who cannot drink alcohol at all. They have a disease. The disease is called alcoholism.

Chapter 5

The Disease Called Alcoholism

In chapter 3 we talked about social drinking. Social drinkers can often control their drinking; they can stop whenever they want to. But social drinkers can sometimes become alcoholics.

Alcoholics have no control over their drinking. They drink to escape from reality. When something unpleasant happens to them, they get drunk to avoid dealing with it. If you keep avoiding your problems instead of dealing with them, your life can completely fall apart. Only you can make decisions about your life. They come from inside of you, not inside of a bottle.

When Teens Drink

Drinking can cause many problems for teens. They cannot concentrate on anything, including schoolwork, if they have been drinking.

Taking a drink does not help anyone solve their problems.

Drinking causes some teens to have run-ins with the law. They get into trouble because of vandalism or drunken driving.

Drinking can lead to alcoholism for teens too. Anyone can become an alcoholic.

Alcoholism and the Alcoholic

Health experts believe that problem drinking leads to alcoholism.

Alcoholism is a **chronic illness**. It is long-lasting. That means that alcoholics must stop drinking alcohol in order to be cured. And they can never drink again if they want to stay well.

Alcoholism creates problems for the drinker, the drinker's family, friends, coworkers, and neighbors. It has affected many lives.

Stages of Alcoholism

Alcoholism usually takes from five to seven years to develop. The disease is **progressive**. It develops in stages. The alcoholic goes through one stage at a time, over a long period of time. Most alcoholics pass through all of the stages. Some alcoholics may not act in all the ways described in each stage. If the descriptions match the behavior of anyone you know, the person may be on the way to becoming an alcoholic. Or he or she may already be an alcoholic. Do any of them describe you, or someone you know? You can get help. See chapter 6.

Stages of Alcoholism

First Stage (Warning Stage)

Drinks too much to feel good.
Drinks to get rid of stress.
Goes from an occasional drink to daily drinks.
Finds reasons to have a drink.
Drinks more each time.
Gets used to more alcohol in the body.

Second Stage (Danger Stage)

- Wants more alcohol.
- Becomes drunk more often.
- Blacks out occasionally, not remembering what happened.
- Drinks alone.
- Sneaks drinks.
- Gulps drinks.
- Feels guilty about drinking.
- Misses work (or school).

Third Stage (Losing Control Stage)

- Blames others for needing drink.
- Withdraws, rejects other people and shuts them out.
- Gets drunk often.
- Blacks out often.
- Spends money recklessly.
- Ignores responsibilities.
- Needs occasional hospitalization because of drinking.

Fourth Stage (Loss of Control Stage)

- Takes any kind of drug.
- Stops making excuses.
- Gets comfort from being drunk.
- Shakes.
- Fails at simple tasks.
- Faces death.

Who Is an Alcoholic?

Anyone can be an alcoholic. It does not matter whether a person is rich or poor, an employed executive or an unemployed laborer, male or female, old or young. Alcoholism may be hereditary (passed on through the family). Studies show that more than half of today's alcoholics had at least one alcoholic parent, grandparent, or other close relative.

There are teenage alcoholics. Teens often start to drink alcohol early enough to be alcoholics by the time they reach high school.

Signs of Alcoholism

Signs of alcoholism are easy to spot during the time it takes for the disease to develop. The following questions highlight some of the early signs of alcoholism. They can help you find out if you or someone you know has a problem with alcohol.

- Do you drink alone?
- Do you sneak a drink in the morning?
- Do you feel that you *need* a drink?
- Do you ever become irritable when you drink?
- Do you drink to get drunk?
- Has your drinking harmed your family or friends in any way?
- Does your drinking change your personality, creating a "new" you?

Sneaking a drink may be an early sign of alcoholism.

- Are you more excited about doing things when you are drinking?
- Do you drink to enjoy parties?
- Does drinking make you moody?
- Have you ever lost your memory (blacked out) when drinking?

Alcoholism: A Character Weakness or a Disease?

Health experts do not agree on what causes alcoholism. They are looking for solid answers to their questions about alcoholism.

For many years the drinker was blamed for alcoholism. People thought an alcoholic had a weak will, a poor character, or low values. Even today, some people argue that alcoholism is simply the result of "willful misconduct." They assert that an alcoholic can correct his or her behavior without help. They think that drinking or not drinking is a matter of discipline.

However, most health experts today call alcoholism a disease. This means that alcoholism, like most other illnesses, must be treated medically.

Recognizing alcoholism as a sickness is a step forward. It means that alcoholics do not have to be ashamed of the problem, nor do people who have an alcoholic parent, husband, or wife. Recognizing the disease and getting early treatment can make an important difference. Alcoholics can recover and return to a full life. But most alcoholics need help in order to recover. Both physical and emotional help are important. Support from family and friends can make a big difference. They can give a recovering alcoholic courage and hope.

Organizations like Alcoholics Anonymous can help people who have drinking problems.

Chapter 6

The Treatment of Alcoholism

A disease is a sickness that eats away at a living thing. When one disease affects many people, it can eat away at an entire part of society. Alcoholism has done a great deal of damage to American society.

Not only are billions of dollars spent to research and perfect medical treatments, but alcoholism has destroyed many lives.

Help in Sight

If you think that you or someone you know may have a drinking problem, it is important to find help. Professional treatment is often the only way someone can quit drinking.

Many hospitals have clinics to help alcoholics. Some special hospitals and homes treat only alcoholics. Some treatment centers are residential. The alcoholic must live there during the treatment. But these are often very expensive. Other treatment centers hold programs during the day or evening. Patients can live at home and continue to work if they are able.

What Is the Treatment for Alcoholism?

An alcoholic *can* stop drinking. But the alcoholic must have treatment. Each patient must find a treatment that works for him or her. Doctors, priests or ministers, and health and social workers can help alcoholics decide what kind of treatment will be best for them.

Detoxification is an important step in the treatment of alcoholism. This process gets rid of all alcohol in the body. After detoxification, the physical need for alcohol is gone, as long as the person doesn't drink again.

Detoxification is usually done in a hospital. This is because a person can suffer tremors, hallucinations, and mental stress during withdrawal from alcohol.

Even after detoxification, it is very hard for an alcoholic to stay away from alcohol. Most treatment centers tell their patients never to have another alcoholic drink. The only way for them to live well and stay healthy is to avoid alcohol completely. One drink, and its effect on the body, can mean the return of the person's dependence on alcohol.

Treatment centers teach the alcoholic how to live without alcohol. They can help "problem drinkers" too. These are people who are not physically dependent on alcohol, but who drink a lot and drink often. The problem drinker learns that he or she can handle problems, have fun, be social, relax, make friends, and feel good about himself or herself *without* alcohol.

Alcoholics Anonymous

This famous self-help organization for alcoholics was founded in 1935 by two alcoholics. They helped each other when they couldn't get help anywhere else. They started Alcoholics Anonymous by talking each other into staying sober one day at a time. Alcoholics Anonymous, called AA for short, helps people who want to stop drinking. It helps them stay away from alcohol.

AA members meet in groups. Members admit their problems to each other and talk about their experiences with alcoholism. In return, the group gives them understanding and support.

There are about thirty-four thousand AA groups in the United States. If you think joining AA could help someone you know, tell him or her about it. The phone number of the group nearest you is listed in the telephone book.

Chapter 7

Other Problems with Alcohol

Many adults today try to be more responsible about drinking and cutting down on their alcohol intake. The same is often not true for teens. More than three million alcoholics in the United States are between the ages of twelve and seventeen. But many teens who do not drink still have a problem with alcohol.

Know the Facts

Seven million young people (under the age of twenty) live with an alcoholic. Sixty percent of all cases of child abuse involve alcohol, and alcoholic families pay twice as much for health care as other families. You may be living with a parent or another member of your family who is addicted to alcohol. In the United States, eighteen million adults are problem drinkers. One family in four has been troubled by alcohol.

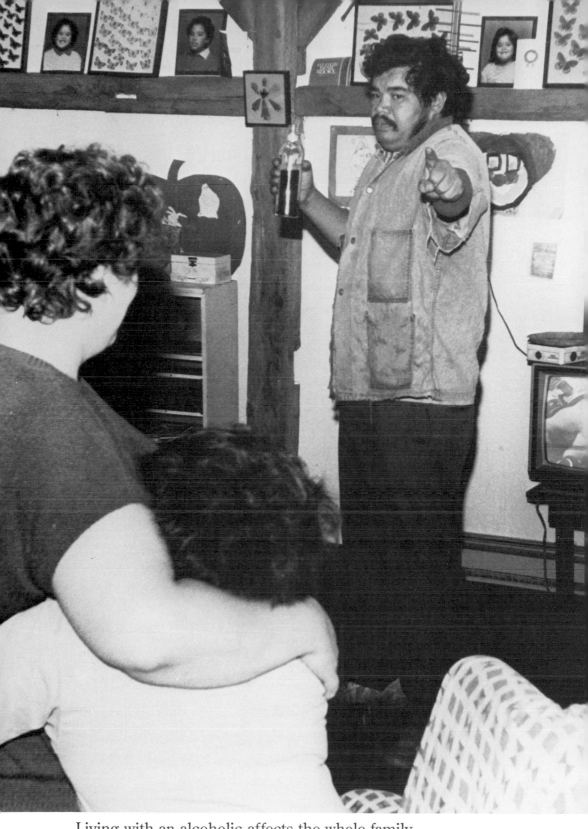

Living with an alcoholic affects the whole family.

Family Under Stress

Alcoholism is often a family illness. Every person in the family is affected. Often a family has problems before a family member becomes an alcoholic. Here are some of the problems an alcoholic's family must cope with:

• Alcoholics may change their moods quickly. They can be laughing or happy one minute and angry or mean the next.
• The alcoholic may spend money irresponsibly or lose his or her job. This may cause money problems for the whole family.
• Alcoholics are often abusive. The abuse can be verbal, physical, or even sexual. If you are abused by an alcoholic in the family, find help fast. Keep telling adults until someone listens.
• Alcoholics may pass out or be sick often. They may not be able to get themselves home when they drink. They may be injured or even killed while driving drunk.
• The alcoholic expects the rest of the family to "cover up" for him or her. The family may not want to go out or have visitors. The family may become unfriendly and isolated.

Members of an alcoholic's family often feel guilty. Sometimes they think the problem is their fault. They feel they should be able to help solve the problem. They wish family life could go back to what it was before alcohol entered their lives.

If someone in your family is an alcoholic, try to be supportive and helpful. But you should not feel guilty if you cannot help someone you love to recover from alcoholism. It is a disease. And it is that person's problem—a problem only he or she can solve.

Alcoholism in the Family

Carley was in a good mood when she got off the school bus. The drama teacher had asked her to try out for a part she wanted in the school play.

But as Carley reached her street, her mood darkened. She felt her stomach muscles tighten. From the outside, her house looked fine, but inside was another story. Carley never knew from day to day what her mother would be like when she got home.

"Why are you so late?" her mother screamed from the living room when Carley stepped inside.

It took Carley some time to spot her mother in the dark living room. She was sitting in the corner, still in her bathrobe. She was holding a glass and the remote control for the TV.

"I've been waiting for you to fix this remote. It doesn't work! It never did." She flung the remote across the room. "And dinner," she yelled. "It should have been started an hour ago."

"I'll get to it. But first I'll fix the TV for you." Carley picked up the remote control. Then she turned on the TV. Her mother had not done that.

Carley ran out of the room. She didn't want to say

A child may feel responsible for an alcoholic parent.

something she would regret. How could she ever bring a date into the house? How could she stand the embarrassment of someone's meeting her mother? How could she find time for play rehearsals? Her mother needed her.

At school the next day Carley went to rehearsal, but she wondered why she bothered. "You're one of the best students I've had," Mr. Burke told Carley. "You really are talented." Carley started to cry. "I don't think I can be in the play," she stammered.

Then she ran out of the classroom.

That night Carley sat alone at the dinner table, eating a roll and a cup of canned soup. She wished she could talk to her mother about what had happened. But earlier her mother had stumbled up the stairs to pass out on her bed.

The doorbell rang. Carley froze. Would her mother wake up and want to come downstairs? Carley ran to get the door before a second ring. Mr. Burke was at the door.

"May I come in?" he asked. Carley stared. "Yes, come in," she managed to say, remembering her manners.

"Where's your mom?" he asked.

"Ah, she . . . she's in bed. She isn't feeling well," Carley stumbled.

"Nothing serious, I hope?" Mr. Burke asked. "I thought the three of us could pick up where we left off when you ran out this afternoon. You see, I don't believe you want to drop out of the play."

"I do," Carley blurted out angrily. "And Mom doesn't want to talk to you about me. She doesn't care about me or about anything these days."

There was a long pause. Then Mr. Burke asked, "Does she drink?"

"Mom? Drink? Yes, a little," Carley said softly, surprised at her honesty. She stared at the floor. "She started drinking when Dad died. I guess raising me alone was tough. Lonely. I tried, but I couldn't take his place."

"Her drinking has nothing to do with you or your

dad, Carley. I knew your mom when your dad was alive. Even then I thought she had a disease. It's called alcoholism. She needs help."

"You mean a doctor?" Carley asked. "In a hospital?"

"For sure a doctor, and maybe a hospital," Mr. Burke said. "I can help you talk to her. As for you, you need help too. You can go with my son Mark to his next meeting. He belongs to a special support group for children of alcoholics. There are a lot of kids your age in the group. They'll help you understand the problems you have living with an alcoholic. You can solve the problems."

"Did you say I could go with Mark, your son?"

"Yes. Not many people know it, but Mark has parents who are recovering alcoholics—my wife and I. Mark has found out that drinkers can get help."

Help for the Family of an Alcoholic

If you live with an alcoholic, you should know that you are not alone with your problems. Many people live with problem drinkers.

Fortunately, help is available for these people. Two help groups have grown out of Alcoholics Anonymous. One is Al-Anon, a support group for the family. Another is Alateen, a support group for children of alcoholics.

Al-Anon helps the wives and husbands of alcoholics. Al-Anon meetings help members deal with the alcoholic's problems and their own problems.

Support groups can help people who live with alcoholics.

Alateen helps young people understand their parents' problems and the disease of alcoholism.

Alcoholics Anonymous, Al-Anon, and Alateen keep their memberships and attendance at meetings private. This means that people can seek help without being embarrassed.

Family Support

The reaction of the alcoholic's family to the problems caused by alcohol affects the alcoholic. Support of family members is important to the treatment of an alcoholic and his or her recovery. An alcoholic needs help and support to deal with the disease.

Here are some ways members of an alcoholic's

family can cope with the problems brought on by
alcohol:

- Learn as much as you can about alcohol and its
  use.
- Learn as much as you can about the disease of
  alcoholism.
- Think about how you feel about alcoholism.
- Try to understand how the alcoholic you know
  is affecting your life.
- Attend Al-Anon or Alateen meetings to learn
  from the experiences of others.
- Discuss your problems with someone you
  trust—a counselor, a doctor, a priest, a rabbi, or
  a minister.
- Remember that you are not the cause of the
  problem.
- Remember that alcoholism is a disease from
  which a person can recover.

Are You in the Know?

We hope that after you have read this book you
have a better understanding of what drinking alcohol is all about. You know the risks involved with
drinking. Keep this in mind the next time you are
tempted to drink. Remember that you don't need
alcohol to have a good time.

Glossary—*Explaining New Words*

abstinence Refraining from doing something.

abuse To use something wrongly.

addict One who is dependent upon alcohol or another drug.

Al-Anon Group of wives and husbands of alcoholics who meet to discuss alcoholism and how to help their alcoholic spouses.

Alateen Group of teenage children of alcoholics who meet to learn about the disease of alcoholism and about how to help themselves and their families.

alcoholic Person suffering from the disease of alcoholism.

alcoholic beverage Any drink that is at least two percent alcohol.

Alcoholics Anonymous Worldwide nonprofit organization that helps people who want to stop drinking alcoholic beverages.

alcoholism Disease in which the body depends on alcohol and the drinker loses control when using alcohol.

blackout Period of time when a drinker cannot remember what happened during or after drinking alcohol.

cirrhosis Disease, often associated with alcoholism, in which the liver and sometimes the kidneys become scarred and hardened.

depressant   Drug that slows down the body.

detoxification   Treatment for alcoholism in which the patient's body is made free of alcohol.

drunkenness   State of temporary partial loss of control over the body due to a high level of alcohol intake.

DWI   Driving while intoxicated; drunk driving.

hereditary characteristic   Characteristic that runs in a family.

intoxication   Drunkenness.

kidneys   Two bean-shaped organs that take in liquid waste from the body and pass it out in urine.

liver   Large organ in the body that helps digest food.

oxidation   The joining of a substance with oxygen.

problem drinker   A person who misuses alcohol.

Prohibition   A law of the United States from 1920 to 1933 that made illegal the sale, manufacture, and transportation of alcoholic beverages.

reflexes   Involuntary movements of the body; movements that occur without thought or effort, such as when a finger touches a hot stove.

sober   Not under the influence of alcohol.

social drinker   A person who drinks alcohol with other people to be social.

Where to Go for Help

Al-Anon/Alateen
600 Corporate Landing
  Parkway
Virginia Beach, VA 23454
(800) 356-9996

Alcoholics Anonymous
  (AA)
National Headquarters
P.O. Box 459, Grand Central
  Station
New York, NY 10163
(212) 870-3400
e-mail:
76245-2153@compuserve.com

Mothers Against Drunk
  Driving (MADD)
511 East John Carpenter
  Freeway, Suite 700
Irving, TX 75062-8187
(214) 744-6233

National Clearinghouse for
  Alcohol and Drug
  Information
P.O. Box 2345
Rockville, MD 20847-2345
(301) 468-2600
e-mail:
info@prevline.health.org
web site:
http://www.health.org

Students Against Driving
  Drunk (SADD)
Box 800
Marlboro, MA 01750
(508) 481-3568

Students to Offset Peer
  Pressure (STOPP)
P.O. Box 103, Department S
Hudson, NH 03051-0103

CANADA

Al-Anon/Alateen
(800) 443-4525

Alcoholics Anonymous
  (AA)
#502, Intergroup Office
234 Enlington Avenue E.
Toronto, ON M4P 1K5
(416) 487-5591

Mothers Against Drunk
  Driving (MADD)
Canadian National Office
6507C Mississauga Road
Toronto, ON L5N 1A6
(905) 813-6233

For Further Reading

Anderson, Peggy King. *Safe At Home!* New York: Atheneum, 1992.

Carter, Alden R. *Up Country.* New York: Putnam, 1989.

Cormier, Robert. *We All Fall Down.* Thorndike, ME: Thorndike Press, 1993.

Ferry, Charles. *Binge.* Rochester, MI: Daisy Hill Press, 1992.

Grant, Cynthia D. *Shadow Man.* New York: Atheneum; Toronto: Maxwell Macmillan Canada; New York: Maxwell Macmillan International, 1992.

Hjelmeland, Andy, and Beckelman, Laurie, eds. *Drinking and Driving.* New York: Crestwood House, 1990.

Shuker, Nancy. *Everything You Need to Know About an Alcoholic Parent*, rev. ed. New York: Rosen Publishing Group, 1995.

Index

About the Author
Barbara Taylor is a writer/editor at Weekly Reader in
Middletown, Connecticut. She has taught in Japan, France,
and Germany as well as in elementary classrooms in
Massachusetts.

About the Editor
Evan Stark is a well-known sociologist, educator, and thera-
pist as well as a popular lecturer on women's and children's
health issues. Dr. Stark was a Henry Rutgers Fellow at
Rutgers University, an associate at the Institution for Social
and Policy Studies at Yale University, and a Fulbright
Fellow at the University of Essex. He is the author of many
publications in the field of family relations and is the father
of four children.

Acknowledgments and Photo Credits
Pp. 11, 12, 33, 36 by Sonja Kalter; p. 40 by Lauren Piperno
all other photos, Stuart Rabinowitz.

Design/Production
Blackbirch Graphics, Inc.

Cover Photograph
Stuart Rabinowitz